12 SUPER-CAMOUFLAGED ANIMALS
YOU NEED TO KNOW

by Nancy Furstinger

12 STORY LIBRARY

www.12StoryLibrary.com

12-Story Library is an imprint of Peterson Publishing Company and Press Room Editions.

Produced for 12-Story Library by Red Line Editorial

Photographs ©: dantemaisto/iStockphoto, cover, 1; Alain Couillaud/iStockphoto, 4; Brandon Alms/iStock/Thinkstock, 5; Frank Leung/iStockphoto, 6, 28; Rose Mary Bush/iStockphoto, 7; ca2hill/iStockphoto, 8; John Pitcher/iStockphoto, 9; reptiles4all/iStockphoto, 10; dennisvdw/iStockphoto, 11; Dennis Donohue/iStockphoto, 12; Dirk Freder/iStockphoto, 13; irvingnsaperstein/iStockphoto, 14; ekvals/iStockphoto, 15; Fotmen/iStockphoto, 16, 29; Marholev/iStockphoto, 17; ymgerman/iStockphoto, 18; elf0724/iStockphoto, 19; impr2003/iStockphoto, 20; Tom Reichner/Shutterstock Images, 21; John Anderson Photo/iStockphoto, 22; Henner Damke/Shutterstock Images, 23; Oktay Ortakcioglu/iStockphoto, 24; i.fario/iStockphoto, 25; Midwest Wilderness/iStockphoto, 26; Steve Oehlenschlager/Shutterstock Images, 27

ISBN
978-1-63235-135-7 (hardcover)
978-1-63235-177-7 (paperback)
978-1-62143-229-6 (hosted ebook)

Library of Congress Control Number: 2015934272

Printed in the United States of America
Mankato, MN
June, 2015

12 STORY LIBRARY

Go beyond the book. Get free, up-to-date content on this topic at 12StoryLibrary.com.

TABLE OF CONTENTS

CHAMELEONS BLEND INTO THEIR SURROUNDINGS

Chameleons are the superstars of camouflage. These lizards can change colors. How do chameleons do this? They have layers of special colored cells under their clear outer skin. When these cells expand or shrink, the chameleon changes color.

Chameleons change color because of light and temperature. They turn a lighter color by reflecting sunlight. This helps their bodies cool down. Chameleons turn a darker color to warm up by absorbing more sunlight.

Many animals use camouflage to blend in with their surroundings. Then they can hunt food or avoid predators. Chameleons change color to signal their moods. A calm chameleon might be green, while an angry one might turn red or yellow to warn others away. Top males show off bright colors to attract females, while shy males display dull colors such as gray. Females turn bright colors to reject males. However, when they do not turn bright colors they are ready to accept males.

Chameleons respond to temperature and their surroundings by changing color.

20

**Amount of time,
in seconds, it takes
a chameleon to
change colors.**

- Most hatchlings start
out as a pastel shade
of green.
- Males are usually more
colorful than females.
- If you time it right, you
can actually watch a
chameleon change
colors.

THINK ABOUT IT

What experiment would
you design to learn how a
chameleon changes color?
Decide what questions you
want your experiment to
answer. Then list the steps you
would take to gather answers.

Chameleons live in Africa, Asia,
India, and Madagascar. The tiny
pygmy chameleon measures
0.9 inches (2.3 cm). This chameleon
fits on a fingertip. The Parson's
chameleon grows up to 27 inches
(69 cm) long. That is approximately
the size of a cat.

There
are nearly 160
different species
of chameleons.

A 360-DEGREE VIEW

Chameleons can rotate their eyes separately. Then they can
look up and down at the same time! Their eyes give them a
360-degree view all around their body. This helps them find
insects that they grab with their long tongues.

COYOTES BECOME NEARLY INVISIBLE TO PREY

Coyotes are skilled at using clever tricks to capture prey. These sly members of the dog family have thick fur that varies from grayish brown to yellowish gray. This makes coyotes difficult to see against their natural surroundings.

Coyotes form family groups called packs. The parents and pups can adjust easily to changes and new conditions. They have expanded their range throughout North America. Coyotes live in many habitats, such as prairies, deserts, forests, and mountains. They have even moved into cities and suburban backyards.

Camouflage is one reason that coyotes have become successful predators. Coyotes become nearly invisible by blending into their environment. This helps them stalk small prey such as mice, squirrels,

Coyotes' fur color depends on their habitat.

COYOTE COMMUNICATION

Coyotes sing in a nighttime chorus. One long howl calls the pack together. Then the pack celebrates by yipping and yelping. Short barks warn pack members of danger and tell enemies to keep away. Females use a high-pitched bark to call their pups.

40

Speed, in miles per hour (64 km/h), at which coyotes can run.

- The US Army uses a camouflage color called "Coyote Brown 498."
- Coyotes' coats blend into a wide range of environments.
- Coyotes living in the mountains have coats containing more shades of gray and black than those living in the desert.

turkeys, and rabbits. They also use sharp vision and a strong sense of smell to find their meals.

Coyotes range in weight from 20 to 50 pounds (9.1 to 23 kg). This is approximately the size of a medium dog. However, coyote tracks differ from those of dogs. When they run, coyotes place their back feet into the prints made by their front feet. This helps them save energy.

Once they locate food, coyotes pounce on their prey.

GREAT GRAY OWLS SWOOP THROUGH THE TREES

Great gray owls blend into the bark of trees in North American forests. This giant owl's wingspan can measure up to five feet (1.5 m), the biggest of any American owl. The great gray owl is mostly made up of feathers. Its thick feathers provide insulation. The owl has white, gray, and brown patterned feathers. It has a pattern resembling a white bowtie on its neck.

This predator uses stealth and camouflage to avoid being spotted until it is too late. The great gray owl perches in a tree, watching and listening for prey.

Then the owl silently dives to the ground to capture small mammals. This forest hunter uses its keen sense of hearing to zero in on rodents.

The owl's yellow eyes are circled with several black-tipped rings.

Great gray owls plunge feet first into the snow to grab their prey.

When it is time to lay eggs in April or May, great gray owls use the abandoned nests of other raptors. Female owls hatch anywhere from two to nine eggs, depending on how much food is available. They lay more eggs when there is an abundance of mice. Males roost in nearby trees, ready to deliver food when hungry females signal them by chirping.

0.5

Distance, in miles (0.8 km), at which a great gray owl's hoot can be heard.

- Light and dark patterns on feathers help owls disappear into tree trunks.
- The owl's markings and feathers help to break up their shape and camouflage them.
- Feathers on the owl's face direct sounds toward their ear openings.

LEAF-TAILED GECKOS HIDE IN THE TREE BRANCHES

The leaf-tailed gecko has some of the most unusual camouflage in the animal kingdom. This lizard is brown or green with patterns and textures that mimic tree bark or moss. The gecko's notched tail is wide and flat.

During the day, the leaf-tailed gecko is nearly invisible. Predators such as owls, rats, and snakes have a difficult time spotting the lizard. When night falls, the gecko hunts. Sticky scales under their toes and curved claws allow geckos to move through the trees and search for meals. Bugs, spiders, and worms are on the menu for this carnivore.

These unusual geckos can only be found in the forests of Madagascar, an island off the coast of Africa. Eight species ranging in size from 4 to 12 inches (10 to 30 cm) live on the island. The tiniest is the satanic leaf-tailed gecko, which is smaller than a dime. This gecko is named for its tiny horns and red eyes!

Leaf-tailed geckos do not have eyelids. When they hide in decayed leaves, dust irritates their eyes. Then these lizards shoot out their long tongues to clean their eyes!

The leaf-tailed gecko's tail resembles a dead leaf.

The gecko soaks up sun among dead leaves and tree branches.

7

Number of US zoos that have satanic leaf-tailed geckos in their collections.

- This gecko's tail looks like insects have nibbled it, helping it blend into foliage.
- Missing chunks of the tail make it resemble a rotten leaf.
- The satanic leaf-tailed gecko's skin contains veins that mimic leaves.

LEOPARDS VANISH AT DUSK

Leopards can hide in plain sight thanks to a spotted pattern that provides camouflage. Spots help these big cats blend in with the shaded regions where they live. Then leopards disappear into the background.

Nine subspecies of leopards live in Africa, Asia, and India. Most are light colored with dark rose-shaped spots called rosettes. African leopards that live in warm dry regions have buff or tawny coats; those living in forests have coats with darker shades. Snow leopards roam the high mountains of Central Asia. Their pale gray or white coats have spots of black and brown. Clouded leopards, named after the cloud-shaped brown spots on their gray or yellow coats, blend into their forest homes in Southeast Asia. Black leopards nearly vanish into the dark tropical rain forests of Asia.

Snow leopards' coats help them blend in with rocks and snow.

THINK ABOUT IT

Spots help big cats such as leopards, cheetahs, and jaguars disappear into their environments. What other patterns might help predators blend in so they can become successful hunters?

450

Population of snow leopards remaining in Pakistan.

- Leopards living in East Africa have circular rosettes, but those in southern Africa have square-shaped spots.
- Spots help leopards blend into patches of light and shadow.
- Scientists are using GPS tracking collars to learn more about leopards' behavior and habitats.

Leopards hunt in the dim light of dusk and dawn. Their spotted camouflage is crucial to their survival. Leopards hide in trees and wait for prey to wander nearby. Then they launch a surprise attack. They pounce down on small hoofed mammals including deer, gazelles, and impalas.

Leopards are athletic animals. They can run at speeds of more than 36 miles per hour (60 km/h). Leopards can leap distances of 20 feet (6.1 m). They are great swimmers. And they can drag prey twice their weight up a tree to keep it safe from hyenas and other scavengers.

Leopards are strong climbers and use trees for hunting, sleeping, and eating.

POLAR BEARS HUNT FOR PREY

Polar bears have snowy fur that helps them blend into their Arctic habitat. Although their fur appears white, it is actually colorless. Guard hairs in the outer layer are hollow. They do not contain any pigment. Beneath their fur, however, polar bears have black skin that can soak up the sun's warmth. Their fur reflects the light so you cannot see the black skin.

Polar bears also have black noses. They cover their noses with their

Polar bears' hollow hairs reflect light.

paws so they can be nearly invisible when they hunt for seals and fish. They wait above breathing holes for seals to surface or the bears wade into the water to hunt.

Polar bears are huge. Males can weigh up to 1,200 pounds (544 kg). Females weigh up to 650 pounds (295 kg). Polar bears measure up to five feet (1.5 m) at the shoulder with all four paws on the ground. Males stretch more than 10 feet tall (3 m) when standing on their hind legs!

Polar bears are the largest land predator.

BUILT FOR AN ARCTIC CLIMATE

Polar bears need to survive temperatures that can plunge to -50 degrees Fahrenheit (-45° C). A thick layer of fat keeps polar bears warm as they hunt for seals. Small ears and a short tail help prevent heat loss. Their furry feet have bumps that let them grip the ice without slipping. Polar bears' claws grasp the snow similar to ice picks.

8

Amount of time, in months, that pregnant polar bears can survive without food.

- Clear tubes of hair make polar bears' fur appear white.
- Polar bears' natural environment is completely white, so they always blend in.
- Some polar bears in zoos have green-tinged fur due to algae growth in the bear pond.

THE PRAYING MANTIS SENSES MOVEMENT

Praying mantises are masters of camouflage. Many of these insects are green or brown. Their coloring helps them to look similar to leaves, stems, tree bark, thorns, or twigs. Other species have more exotic colors. The bright pink or yellow orchid mantis looks similar to a flower petal.

Praying mantises are fierce predators. They blend in among plants and flowers in order to ambush their prey. They launch a surprise attack on crickets, flies, grasshoppers, and moths.

When the praying mantis is resting, its forelegs appear to be folded in prayer. The mantis is the only insect that can rotate its head 180 degrees to search for a meal. Compound eyes, which are made up of many separate visual units, help these

There are many different colored praying mantises.

insects sense movements. When the praying mantis spots prey, it uses amazing speed and spiked front legs to trap its meal. Then it pins down its prey and eats it alive.

The praying mantis uses tricks of color and shape to hide from predators. If a bird or lizard finds this insect, the mantis fans its wings. This makes it appear more threatening. The mantis will also stand up on its back legs and spread its forelegs to look larger.

200
Number of nymphs that can hatch from one egg case.

- The praying mantis' flat, triangular shape mimics the leaves it sits on.
- Camouflage helps this insect avoid the attention of predators and also allows it to attack its prey.
- Egg cases resemble Styrofoam and shield eggs during the winter.

The praying mantis is named for its posture.

SEA DRAGON HIDES IN SEAWEED

Camouflage is vital for the two species of sea dragons that live off the coast of Australia. Leafy sea dragons range in color from brown to yellow. Their bodies are decorated with olive leaf-shaped appendages. Weedy sea dragons are red with yellow spots. Their feathery fins help them blend into the sea floor.

Sea dragons use their disguises to hunt. They sway like sea plants so prey does not detect them. Both species are carnivores. Their long, thin snouts look similar to pipes. The snouts are built to suck in tiny sea animals, such as shrimp and small fish.

The leafy sea dragon's body helps it disappear into its seaweed home.

Sea dragons use their bodies to quickly move through the water.

Sea dragons look similar to underwater dragons. These fish are covered in hard bony plates. They have small heads, slender bodies, and huge tails. The leafy sea dragons grow up to 14 inches (36 cm) in length. The weedy sea dragon grows up to 18 inches (46 cm) long. Both species of sea dragons propel themselves through the water using fins near their neck and tail.

5

Percentage of sea dragons that live to be two years old.

- Since sea dragons are masters of camouflage, predators rarely eat them.
- Leafy sea dragons blend into their environment by changing colors.
- Weedy sea dragons sway with the currents to resemble sea grasses.

DEDICATED DADS

Male sea dragons are pregnant fathers! During mating, the female lays up to 300 bright pink eggs in a pouch on the underside of the male's tail. The father-to-be carries the eggs for two months. Then he pumps his tail until all the babies hatch. The tiny sea dragons look like miniature adults.

SNOWSHOE HARES CHANGE COLOR WITH THE SEASONS

Snowshoe hares have fur that changes color. This keeps them camouflaged in all seasons. From spring through fall, these hares are a reddish brown to blend in with rocks and dirt. In the winter, they transform to pure white to match their snowy environment.

The color change helps protect snowshoe hares from predators. They have a better chance of survival when they disappear into their background. Owls, coyotes, lynx, and foxes have a difficult time discovering the hares.

Unlike rabbits that freeze when threatened, hares race away from danger. They can sprint up to 27 miles per hour (43 km/h).

These athletic animals can also leap 10 feet (3 m) in a single bound!

Snowshoe hares live in coniferous forests in Canada and the northern United

Snowshoe hares have black ear tips year round.

Snowshoe hares eat grasses during the summer months.

States. Winters are very long, so the hare has adapted to survive the cold. Thick fur provides insulation. Short ears also help reduce heat loss. And large hind feet act as snowshoes, helping spread weight over a larger area so hares can walk on top of the snow.

Like their fur color, the diet of snowshoe hares also changes with the seasons. Leafy greens such as grasses, ferns, and clovers are on the menu in the summer. In the winter, the hare nibbles woody plants such as maple, balsam, birch, spruce, and willow.

3

Number of litters a female snowshoe hare has each year.

- It takes approximately ten weeks for the snowshoe hare's coat to completely change color.
- The pineal gland, located in the hare's brain, signals when to change coat color based on changes in daylight lengths.
- Snowshoe hares are nicknamed the "varying hare" due to their seasonal color change.

STONEFISH CONCEALS ITSELF ON THE SEA FLOOR

The stonefish could win an award for best disguise. This fish hides on the sea floor of shallow tropical waters, such as the Indian and Pacific oceans. By burrowing in the mud or sand, it resembles the rocks and coral in its surroundings. The stonefish is brown or gray with bumps of yellow, orange, or red. It grows 14 to 20 inches (36 to 51 cm) in length.

This fish is a patient hunter. It might stay in the same spot for days. The stonefish waits for prey such as small fish and shrimp to swim nearby. Then the stonefish strikes with amazing speed. The stonefish opens its mouth and sucks in its victim similar to a vacuum. It is so fast that a special high-speed camera is needed to show the stonefish in action!

The stonefish has a deadly weapon that makes it the most venomous fish in the world. Thirteen spines

The stonefish can be very hard to see in its habitat.

0.015

Time, in seconds, it takes a stonefish to capture its prey.

- Warty skin allows the stonefish to hide in plain sight.
- Since stonefish are so well camouflaged, people are warned to swim rather than walk in shallow coastal waters.
- Unlike some animals such as poison dart frogs, stonefish do not advertise their venom with bright colors.

jut out of the dorsal fin on its back. They contain poisonous venom that the stonefish uses to sting its enemies. The stonefish can kill unlucky people who step on it if they do not seek treatment quickly.

The sting from a stonefish causes intense pain and swelling.

THE WALKING STICK DOES A DISAPPEARING TRICK

The walking stick uses a disappearing trick to confuse its enemies. This insect remains visible but freezes in place. Then it looks exactly like a tree branch that predators would never attempt to eat. The walking stick can even sway back and forth when it walks on its

There are nearly 3,000 species of walking sticks.

OUTSMARTING PREDATORS

Walking sticks have other ways to outsmart predators, too. Some squirt liquid that burns an enemy's eyes and makes it briefly blind. Some release foul-smelling chemicals. Others flash brightly colored wings and then hide their wings and disappear into a pile of brown twigs. Still others are brightly colored to warn enemies that they will discharge stinky fluids if attacked. Some walking sticks use spines on their legs to attack. Others escape enemies by shedding their legs. Later on they can regrow new legs.

It can be easy to miss a walking stick that is on a tree branch.

toothpick legs. Predators think the insect is a twig moving in the breeze.

But one predator is not fooled by the walking stick. Bats are not deceived by the walking stick's disguise. That is because bats use echolocation rather than sight to find a meal.

Most walking sticks are shades of brown or green. They range in size from 0.5 inches to 13 inches (1.3 to 33 cm) long. These insects live in woodlands and tropical forests on every continent except Antarctica.

1,500
Number of eggs laid by a walking stick.

- Walking stick eggs are also camouflaged to look like plant seeds.
- Some walking sticks boast bright colors while others have stripes.
- Other walking sticks have growths on their bodies that resemble tree bark.

THINK ABOUT IT

Brainstorm different ways that walking sticks can avoid becoming meals for predators. Pick one characteristic. Then write a story about how the walking stick escapes its predator.

WHITE-TAILED DEER RACE AWAY FROM ENEMIES

Many baby animals have special camouflage that changes as they grow. Young white-tailed deer, called fawns, have a reddish-brown coat dotted with hundreds of white spots. As fawns grow older, their spots vanish.

Fawns keep completely still during the day while their mothers are out hunting for food. Fawns stretch out flat on the ground, waiting for their mothers to return. Their spots allow them to blend into the sunny forest floor. This makes fawns difficult for predators to spot.

Fawns grow quickly. Female deer, called does, and male deer,

Fawns rely on camouflage to protect them.

called bucks, have summer coats of reddish-brown that help them blend into woodlands. This color fades to a grayish-brown in winter, which allows deer to blend in with bare trunks and branches. Bucks also grow a pair of antlers each year. The antlers fall off each winter.

White-tailed deer use speed to race away from predators such as bobcats, coyotes, and mountain lions. They can sprint at speeds of up to 30 miles per hour (48 km/h). They also move with spectacular leaps and bounds. Deer can jump 10 feet (3 m) high and 30 feet (9.1 m) across forest obstacles. As they escape danger, deer display the underside of their tails.

3.5
Average age, in months, of a fawn when it loses its spots.

- Fawns lose their white spots before they molt their summer coats.
- The shadow patterns that sunlight casts when it filters through tree leaves matches the patterns of a fawn's coat.
- If fawns venture into grassy areas, their camouflage is no longer effective.

White-tailed deer wave their tails like white flags to signal others in their herd.

FACT SHEET

- Animals use camouflage to escape predators and ambush prey. This helps them survive in nature. Animals that are smaller and slower than their predators need to match their surroundings so their enemies fail to notice them. Predators use camouflage to sneak up on their prey.

- The devices that animals use to blend into their environments vary. Most use coloration. This pattern of colors could be in the animal's fur, feathers, or scales. Some also use texture to match their surroundings. Their fur might be coarse rather than smooth so they can blend in with tree bark.

- Countershading helps protect sea creatures. In this type of camouflage, the top of the animal's body is a darker color while its underside is lighter. For example, sea turtles have dark shells that, when seen from above, blend into deep ocean waters. When seen from below, their light bottom shells blend in with the bright sky and lighter surface water. This camouflage protects sea turtles from predators both below and above water.

- Some animals change camouflage with the seasons. For example, both snowshoe hares and arctic foxes turn white in the winter to blend in with the snow. In the summer, their fur changes to a reddish brown to match the earth.

- Many insects are masters of disguise. They blend in with their surroundings by using different shapes and textures. They might mimic leaves or twigs to avoid detection.

GLOSSARY

appendage
A projecting part of an animal, such as an antenna or a leg.

camouflage
Coloring or covering that hides or disguises animals so they look like their surroundings.

carnivore
A meat eater.

coniferous
Trees that have needles and produce cones.

dorsal fin
A single fin on the back of a fish that gives it stability while swimming.

echolocation
A method some animals use to locate an object by using an emitted sound and the reflection back from it.

habitat
The place where an animal naturally lives.

hatchling
A very young animal that has just come from the egg.

insulation
Something that prevents or reduces the passage of heat.

molt
To lose a covering of hair or feathers and replace it with new growth.

pigment
A natural substance that gives animal tissue its color.

predator
An animal that preys on others for food.

prey
An animal that is hunted or killed by another for food.

FOR MORE INFORMATION

Books

Berger, Gilda and Melvin. *101 Hidden Animals.* New York: Scholastic, 2014.

Pryor, Kimberley Jane. *Clever Camouflage.* Tarrytown, NY: Marshall Cavendish, 2010.

Stevenson, Emma. *Hide-and-Seek Science: Animal Camouflage.* New York: Holiday House, 2013.

Websites

Discovery: Animal Camouflage Pictures
www.discovery.com/tv-shows/curiosity/topics/animal-camouflage-pictures.htm

National Geographic: Praying Mantises
www.animals.nationalgeographic.com/animals/bugs/praying-mantis

San Diego Zoo: Chameleons
animals.sandiegozoo.org/animals/chameleon

INDEX

About the Author

Nancy Furstinger has been speaking up for animals since she learned to talk. She is the author of nearly 100 books, including many on her favorite topic: animals! She shares her home with big dogs and house rabbits (all rescued). Furstinger also volunteers for several animal organizations.

READ MORE FROM 12-STORY LIBRARY

Every 12-Story Library book is available in many formats, including Amazon Kindle and Apple iBooks. For more information, visit your device's store or 12StoryLibrary.com.